Sassy Cookies

Sweet, Spicy, & Savory Treats with Swagger

By Luane Kohnke
Photographs by John Uher

PELICAN PUBLISHING COMPANY
GRETNA 2013

To Larry.
Thanks, as always, for your patience, encouragement, and support.

The word "Pelican" and the depiction of a pelican
are trademarks of Pelican Publishing Company, Inc.,
and are registered in the U.S. Patent and Trademark Office.

Library of Congress Cataloging-in-Publication Data

Kohnke, Luane.
  Sassy cookies : sweet, spicy, and savory treats with swagger / Luane
Kohnke ; photographs by John Uher.
      pages cm
  Includes index.
  ISBN 978-1-4556-1769-2 (hardcover : alkaline paper) — ISBN 978-
1-4556-1770-8 (e-book) 1. Cookies. 2. Cooking (Spices) 3. Cooking
(Herbs) I. Title.
  TX772.K67 2013
  641.86'54—dc23
                                            2013008128

Printed in China
Published by Pelican Publishing Company, Inc.
1000 Burmaster Street, Gretna, Louisiana 70053

Contents

Acknowledgments and Introduction

Thanks to the dedicated recipe testers who provided important feedback throughout this project: Karen Bonna-Rainert, Christine Como, Beth Goehring, Nadia Schwartz, and Rebecca Wilkins.

Thanks also to my colleagues at R/GA, a digital advertising agency, for eating every sample batch of cookies that I baked, offering comments, and encouraging me to bake, bake, bake. You are an inspiration!

And, of course, thanks to the two men who never let me down, my husband, Larry, and my best friend, Matt. Without you I would be lost.

Baking is pure joy! Creating new recipes brings happiness. Sharing and making others happy is the ultimate satisfaction. I love baking, creating, and sharing. I have been baking since I was nine years old, living on my parents' farm in Wisconsin, and I have been creating new recipes since I was fifteen.

People ask me about the source of my inspiration for new recipes. Honestly, it comes from everywhere—trying new cuisines, reading about food, or talking to friends about their food experiences. Although I own hundreds of cookbooks, mostly I am inspired by a flavor or an ingredient. Then you'll hear me say, "I want to make a cookie with . . . " Yes, that is how it starts: the quest to make a cookie with saffron or lavender or green tea; the mission to recreate the flavor of a coconut-curry-chocolate bar in the form of a cookie; or the realization, based on a lunchtime fennel salad, that anise and pistachio are an interesting pairing. That is where it begins, in some everyday moment.

Sassy Cookies is the culmination of at least forty of those quests to bring to life a new sweet, spicy, or savory idea. It contains an in-depth exploration of chocolate, fruits, nuts, herbs, and cheese. It includes inspirations from Latin America, Europe, and Asia. It provides eight gluten-free creations as well, so that those with gluten sensitivities can enjoy the pleasure of new flavor treats.

I hope that you enjoy baking my creations and that sharing them with your family and friends leads to many happy moments!

Cookie Basics

General Preparation Guidelines

1. About 15 minutes before baking your first batch, preheat your oven to the temperature in the recipe. If using a convection oven, reduce the baking temperature by 25 degrees, and check for doneness a bit earlier than the recipe calls for.

2. When measuring all-purpose flour and any other dry ingredient, scoop the ingredient from its container into the measuring cup or spoon, and scrape off the excess with a straight edge. This will ensure accuracy in your measurements.

3. Sift or whisk the dry ingredients as directed. This technique aerates the flour and distributes the leavening and spices evenly throughout, making the finished cookie more uniform in texture.

4. Most butter and eggs should be at room temperature (about 65 degrees) before beating. Room-temperature butter is pliable but not soft or melted.

5. Dry ingredients are added to the butter mixture just until all traces of the flour disappear. Overmixing develops the gluten in the dough and results in a tough cookie.

6. If instructions call for chilling, chill for the minimum amount of time. Chilling relaxes the gluten and helps flavors become more developed and integrated into the dough. Cookies become more tender and flavorful. Chilling also helps them spread less during baking. If chilled dough is too stiff to scoop or roll, let it soften a few minutes at room temperature.

7. Parchment paper is recommended as a liner for cookie sheets. Cookies will not stick to it, making cleanup easier. Parchment also has an insulating effect, which promotes even baking.

8. Cookies bake more evenly if they are all the same size. I recommend using a cookie scoop to form equal-size dough balls. You can also use a scale to measure equal-size portions.

9. Cool cookies thoroughly before storing in an airtight container. Cookies that are not completely cooled before storing can become soggy

and lose their shape from trapped steam. Store each cookie variety in its own sealed container, so that flavors and aromas don't mingle.

Freezing and Storage Tips

Freezing cookie dough or baked cookies is a great way to manage your time and serve just the quantity you need.

Freezing dough: Most stiff cookie doughs can be frozen. Liquid batters or meringue dough cannot be frozen.

To freeze drop cookies, scoop uniform balls onto a cookie sheet, spacing them 1 inch apart, and freeze them until solid. Put the frozen balls into a freezer storage bag, and store up to 1 month in the freezer. When you are ready to bake, place frozen cookie balls on a prepared cookie sheet, spacing as directed in the recipe, and defrost completely before baking. You can also freeze the entire batch of dough in a sealed plastic container and defrost it in the refrigerator for several hours or overnight, then use as directed.

For slice-and-bake cookie logs, shape and wrap logs in wax paper or plastic wrap, then wrap in foil and place in a freezer storage bag. To defrost, cut the frozen dough into individual slices and defrost, or defrost the entire log, in the refrigerator for several hours or overnight, and use as directed.

Freezing cookies: Be sure the cookies are completely cooled before freezing. Freeze them, layered between wax or parchment paper, in a freezer storage bag. For extra protection, wrap the cookie layers in plastic wrap before putting them into the freezer bag. If the cookies are fragile, place the filled freezer storage bag on a cookie sheet or in a plastic container, to protect the edges of the cookies. Cookies can be stored for up to 1 month in the freezer. To defrost, place cookies in a single layer on a flat surface, and leave at room temperature for about 1 hour.

For bar cookies, cut the pan of cookies into individual cookies and wrap each cookie in plastic wrap. Place the wrapped cookies in a freezer storage bag, and freeze. Alternatively, wrap the entire pan of uncut cookies in plastic wrap or foil, place it in a freezer storage bag, and freeze. Bar cookies can be stored in the freezer for 4 to 6 weeks. To defrost individual bar cookies, place unwrapped cookies in a single layer on a flat surface, and leave at room temperature for about 1 hour. For a pan of uncut cookies, defrost at room temperature for 2 to 3 hours.

Chocolate, Spice, and Everything Nice

Chocolate has a timeless appeal to both simple and sophisticated palates. These chocolate cookies bring new flavor combinations front and center. In this chapter, find something innovative, dazzling, and unexpected to add to your cookie repertoire.

Chocolate Mexican Spice Cookies
Makes 30 to 36 cookies

I am often inspired by flavors in candy bars. One of my favorite chocolate combinations is found in Lindt's chocolate, chili, and cherry bar. These soft, chewy cookies mix cinnamon and cayenne with dark, rich chocolate and tart cherries. To make them extra-dark, substitute 1 tbsp. black cocoa for 1 tbsp. Dutch-process cocoa.

Preheat oven to 350 degrees. Line cookie sheets with parchment paper.

In a medium bowl, sift together flour, cocoa, baking soda, salt, and spices. Set aside.

In the large bowl of an electric mixer, with speed set to high, cream the butter and sugars 2 to 3 minutes, until fluffy. Add egg and vanilla extract. Beat until well combined.

Set mixer to low. Add the flour mixture, and mix until just combined. Fold in chocolate chips and cherries.

Using a medium cookie scoop (#40), drop rounded tablespoons of dough onto prepared cookie sheets, spacing about 2 inches apart. Bake 12 to 14 minutes, until puffed and cracked. Cool on cookie sheets for 2 minutes.

Transfer cookies, still on parchment, to wire racks to cool completely.

Store in an airtight container, at room temperature, for up to 3 days.

INGREDIENTS

¾ cup plus 2 tbsp. all-purpose flour
½ cup plus 2 tbsp. unsweetened Dutch-process cocoa
1 tsp. baking soda
⅛ tsp. sea salt
½ tsp. cinnamon
¼ tsp. cayenne pepper
⅛ tsp. ground black pepper
10 tbsp. (1¼ sticks) unsalted butter, room temperature
½ cup plus 2 tbsp. granulated sugar
¼ cup plus 2 tbsp. packed dark brown sugar
1 large egg, room temperature
½ tsp. pure vanilla extract
6 oz. (about 1 cup) bittersweet or semisweet chocolate chips
¾ cup dried sour cherries, coarsely chopped

Baker's Note: If you prefer the cookie less spicy, reduce the cayenne pepper to ⅛ tsp.

Chocolate-Ginger Fudge Shortbread Cookies
Makes 60 to 72 cookies

Chocolate-ginger fudge is layered over a thin buttery shortbread cookie. For the best results, use Lyle's Golden Syrup or another cane-sugar syrup in the topping. Cut the cookies into 1-inch squares, because a small piece will easily satisfy a sweet tooth.

Preheat oven to 350 degrees. Line the sides and bottom of an 8x8-inch baking pan with foil, leaving an overhang of about 2 inches on each of 2 opposite sides. Cut parchment paper to fit bottom of pan, and place on foil. Lightly butter bottom and sides. Set aside.

In a medium bowl, sift together flour, cornstarch, and salt. Whisk in brown sugar. With a pastry cutter, cut in butter until dough resembles coarse meal. Add water and egg yolk. With a fork, blend until combined.

Spread the dough in a thin, even layer across the bottom of the pan. Smooth top. Bake 15 to 20 minutes, until golden. Pierce crust if it bubbles.

About 2 to 3 minutes before shortbread is done, prepare topping. Melt butter in a small saucepan, and stir in chocolate, golden syrup, powdered sugar, ground ginger, and vanilla until smooth. Fold in crystallized ginger.

Remove shortbread from oven. While shortbread is still warm, spread topping over crust. Smooth top.

Cool completely in the pan. Then, using foil overhang as an aid, lift uncut cookies out of pan, and cut into 1-inch squares.

Store in an airtight container, at room temperature, for up to 5 days.

INGREDIENTS

1 cup all-purpose flour
2 tsp. cornstarch
¼ tsp. salt
¼ cup packed light brown sugar
8 tbsp. (1 stick) chilled unsalted butter, cut
    into ½-inch cubes
1 tbsp. water
1 large egg yolk, room temperature

Topping
8 tbsp. (1 stick) unsalted butter
6 oz. bittersweet or semisweet chocolate
2 tbsp. Lyle's Golden Syrup (or substitute
    light corn syrup)
2 cups powdered sugar
1 tsp. ground ginger
1 tsp. pure vanilla extract
¼ cup chopped crystallized ginger

Baker's Note: For an extra kick, sprinkle 2 tbsp. chopped crystallized ginger onto the warm topping, and press lightly so the pieces adhere.

Chocolate Malt Sandwich Cookies
Makes 54 to 60 unfilled cookies or 27 to 30 sandwich cookies

These dense chocolate malt cookies are perfectly paired with this tangy, crème fraiche and white chocolate ganache filling. They are reminiscent of a chocolate malt with vanilla ice cream. They can also be enjoyed unfilled or served as an accompaniment to a bowl of vanilla ice cream.

Preheat oven to 350 degrees. Line cookie sheets with parchment paper.

In a medium bowl, sift together the flour, baking powder, baking soda, and salt.

In a separate medium bowl, sift together the cocoa and malted-milk powder.

In the large bowl of an electric mixer, with speed set to high, beat eggs about 4 to 5 minutes, until doubled in volume. Add heavy cream and crème fraiche. Beat until thoroughly combined.

Add vanilla and powdered sugar. Beat until thoroughly combined. Add melted chocolate. Beat until combined.

Add cocoa-malted-milk mixture, in 3 or 4 portions, and mix until thoroughly combined. Set mixer speed to low. Mix in flour mixture until combined.

Add chopped semisweet and white chocolate. Mix until combined. Dough will have the consistency of thick frosting.

Using a small cookie scoop (#100), shape dough into ¾-inch balls and drop onto prepared cookie sheets, spacing them about 2 inches apart. Bake 10 to 12 minutes, until firm to the touch. Transfer cookies, still on parchment, to wire racks to cool completely.

To prepare filling, put white chocolate in a small mixing bowl. Set aside.

Put heavy cream in a small saucepan and bring to a boil. Add vanilla and crème fraiche. Stir about 15 seconds, until combined and heated through.

Pour hot cream mixture over chocolate, and stir until smooth. Chill in refrigerator for 30 minutes to 1 hour, stirring occasionally, until mixture becomes thick enough to spread.

When ready to serve, spread ¾ tsp. filling onto the bottom side of a cookie. Place a second cookie, flat side down, on top of the filling, and gently press cookies together. Repeat with remaining cookies.

Store unfilled cookies in an airtight container, at room temperature, for up to 3 days.

INGREDIENTS

6 tbsp. all-purpose flour
¼ tsp. baking powder
⅛ tsp. baking soda
⅛ tsp. salt
¼ cup Dutch-process cocoa
½ cup malted-milk powder
2 large eggs, room temperature
2 tbsp. heavy cream
2 tbsp. crème fraiche
2 tsp. pure vanilla extract
1 cup powdered sugar
2 oz. unsweetened chocolate, melted and cooled
2 oz. semisweet chocolate, chopped
2 oz. white chocolate, chopped

Filling

5 oz. white chocolate, finely chopped
3 tbsp. heavy cream
½ tsp. pure vanilla extract
3 tbsp. crème fraiche

Lemony White Chocolate and Pink Peppercorn Delights
Makes 30 to 36 cookies

Brown sugar and butter caramelize to make these buttery, white chocolate chip cookies crispy on the edges and chewy on the insides. The lemon complements the mild, pink peppercorn spice, leaving a warm mouth feeling. Chill the dough overnight to allow the flavor to fully develop. These are my new favorite.

In a medium bowl, sift together flour, salt, and baking soda. Set aside.

In the large bowl of an electric mixer, with speed set to high, cream butter about 1 minute, until fluffy. Add sugars and egg. Beat about 3 minutes, until light and fluffy.

Add lemon juice, lemon zest, peppercorns, and vanilla. Beat until combined. Reduce speed to low. Add flour mixture, and mix until just combined. Add white chocolate chips, and mix until combined.

Refrigerate overnight for flavors to fully develop.

Preheat oven to 350 degrees. Line cookie sheets with parchment paper.

Using a medium cookie scoop (#40), drop rounded tablespoons of dough onto prepared cookie sheets, spacing them about 2½ inches apart. Bake 12 to 15 minutes, until centers are golden brown and edges are a shade darker. Transfer cookies, still on parchment, to wire racks to cool completely.

Store in an airtight container, at room temperature, for up to 1 week.

INGREDIENTS

1 cup all-purpose flour
½ tsp. salt
¼ tsp. baking soda
8 tbsp. (1 stick) unsalted butter, room temperature
½ cup packed light brown sugar
¼ cup granulated sugar
1 large egg, room temperature
1 tbsp. fresh lemon juice
1 tsp. grated lemon zest, packed
1 tsp. pink peppercorns, crushed
½ tsp. pure vanilla extract
2 cups white chocolate chips

Baker's Note: If you prefer a crispier cookie, bake until tops are a deep golden brown, 15 to 16 minutes.

Mocha Chocolate Wedding Cakes
Makes 30 to 36 cookies

These mocha-chocolate-hazelnut cookies are a not-too-sweet, coffee-flavored variation on polvorones *(Mexican wedding cake cookies). They are delicious sprinkled with a blend of powdered sugar and cocoa.*

Preheat oven to 350 degrees. Line cookie sheets with parchment paper.

In a medium bowl, sift together flour, cocoa, and espresso powder. (If using coffee extract, add as directed below.) Set aside.

In the large bowl of an electric mixer, with speed set to high, beat butter and powdered sugar, about 2 minutes, until pale and fluffy. Add salt and vanilla. If using coffee extract, add. Beat until combined.

Set the mixer speed to low, and add the flour mixture. Mix until just combined. Mix in hazelnuts.

Dough will be crumbly. Gather dough together with hands, and form a smooth mass.

Using a small cookie scoop (#100), shape dough into 1-inch balls and, spacing them about 2 inches apart, drop onto prepared cookie sheets. Bake 10 to 12 minutes, until bottoms are brown. Transfer cookies, still on parchment, to wire racks to cool. Cool cookies 5 to 10 minutes.

Sprinkle with powdered sugar-cocoa mixture, if desired. Cool completely.

Store in an airtight container, at room temperature, for up to 3 days.

INGREDIENTS

1 cup all-purpose flour
2 tbsp. Dutch-process cocoa
1 tsp. instant espresso powder (or substitute ¾ tsp. pure coffee extract)
8 tbsp. (1 stick) unsalted butter, room temperature
¼ cup powdered sugar
⅛ tsp. salt
½ tsp. pure vanilla extract
½ scant cup finely chopped, lightly toasted hazelnuts
½ cup powdered sugar plus 2 tbsp. Dutch-process cocoa, sifted together, for sprinkling (optional)

Chocolate Shortbread and Hazelnut Cream Sandwich Cookies
Makes 18 to 24 sandwich cookies

My friend Karen suggested I combine my signature chocolate shortbread cookies with a delicious hazelnut buttercream filling. Make the filling ahead of time, and assemble the cookies just before serving.

In a medium bowl, sift together flour and cocoa. Whisk in sugar. With a pastry cutter, cut in butter until it resembles flakes.

Knead with hands until gathered together, smooth, and pliable. Shape dough into disk, and wrap in wax paper or plastic wrap. Chill for 1 to 2 hours, or overnight, until firm.

In the small bowl of an electric mixer, with speed set to high, beat together the egg and superfine sugar for 2 to 3 minutes, until light and fluffy. Pour mixture into a saucepan. Add the ground hazelnuts, and heat 1 to 2 minutes over low heat, stirring frequently, until thick and creamy. Place mixture in a small covered bowl, and cool in refrigerator for about 10 minutes.

Clean blades and bowl. With speed set to medium, beat butter until fluffy. Add the chilled hazelnut mixture, beating 1 to 2 minutes until light and fluffy. Store filling in refrigerator, until ready to use.

Preheat oven to 350 degrees. Line cookie sheets with parchment paper.

Roll cookie dough, between sheets of wax paper, to ¼-inch thickness. Cut with 1-inch round cookie cutter, dipping cookie cutter in all-purpose flour to aid cutting. Place cookies on prepared cookie sheets, spacing them about 2 inches apart. If desired, sprinkle half of the cookies with chocolate sprinkles. Leave the others plain. Bake 10 to 12 minutes, until bottoms are lightly browned. Transfer cookies, still on parchment, to wire racks to cool completely.

Just before serving, remove filling from refrigerator. Let sit a few minutes until soft enough to spread. Spread ½ tsp. over flat side of a cookie. Place a second cookie, flat side down, on top of the filling, and gently press cookies together. (If you used sprinkles, be sure to use a plain cookie as the first cookie and a sprinkle-topped cookie as the second cookie.) Repeat with remaining cookies.

Store unfilled cookies in an airtight container, at room temperature, for up to 5 days.

INGREDIENTS

1 cup all-purpose flour
2 tbsp. Dutch-process cocoa
¼ cup granulated sugar
8 tbsp. (1 stick) cold butter, cut into ½-inch cubes
Chocolate sprinkles (optional)

Filling

1 large egg, room temperature
⅓ cup superfine granulated sugar
3 tbsp. finely ground, lightly toasted hazelnuts
4 tbsp. (½ stick) unsalted butter, room temperature

Chai Tea and Chocolate Butter Cookies
Makes 18 to 24 cookies

These tender, chewy butter cookies have a spicy, aromatic taste that is balanced by the addition of high-quality milk chocolate. Use organic chai tea, such as Tazo, in these delicious treats. For a deeper chocolate flavor, substitute semisweet chocolate for milk chocolate.

In a medium bowl, sift together flour, ground chai tea, baking soda, and sea salt. Set aside.

In the large bowl of an electric mixer, with speed set to high, cream butter 1 to 2 minutes, until light and fluffy. Add sugars and egg. Beat 1 to 2 minutes until fluffy.

Add vanilla and orange zest. Mix until well combined. Reduce speed to low, and add flour mixture. Mix until just combined.

Add chopped chocolate. Mix until just combined. Cover and refrigerate at least 2 hours, for flavors to develop.

Preheat oven to 350 degrees. Line cookie sheets with parchment paper.

Using a medium cookie scoop (#40), shape the dough into 1-inch balls. Roll tops in coarse sugar. Place 2 inches apart on prepared cookie sheets.

Bake 10 to 12 minutes, until golden brown. Cool 2 minutes on cookie sheet. Transfer cookies, still on parchment, to wire racks to cool completely.

Store in an airtight container, at room temperature, for up to 5 days.

INGREDIENTS

1 cup all-purpose flour
2 tsp. organic chai tea, finely ground (about 2 teabags)
½ tsp. baking soda
¼ tsp. fine sea salt
8 tbsp. (1 stick) butter, room temperature
½ cup granulated sugar
2 tbsp. packed light brown sugar
1 large egg, room temperature
1 tsp. pure vanilla extract
1 tsp. grated orange zest, packed
4 oz. high-quality milk chocolate, such as Lindt, finely chopped
Coarse raw sugar, such as demerara, for rolling

Baker's Note: A small food processer or nut chopper can be used to grind the tea leaves. Do not use leaves straight from the bag; they will be too large.

Dark-Chocolate Spice Cookies with Ganache Filling
Makes 18 to 24 sandwich cookies

My love for the Naga chocolate bar by Vosges inspired me to develop these spicy, dark-chocolate cookies, flavored with sweet curry and cardamom and sandwiching a filling of chocolate-coconut ganache. Use a sweet curry powder like Penzeys (www.penzeys.com) or Spice House for the best results.

In a medium bowl, sift together flour, cocoa, baking soda, spices, and sea salt. Set aside.

In the large bowl of an electric mixer, with speed set to high, beat butter and sugars 2 to 3 minutes, until light and fluffy. Add vanilla and egg yolk. Beat 1 to 2 minutes, until light and fluffy.

Reduce speed to low. Add flour mixture, and mix until smooth. Shape dough into a disk, and wrap in wax paper or plastic wrap. Refrigerate 1 hour or overnight, until firm.

Preheat oven to 350 degrees. Line cookie sheets with parchment paper.

Roll dough, between sheets of wax paper, to ¼-inch thickness. Cut with a 1-inch round cookie cutter. Place cookies on prepared cookie sheets, spacing them about 2 inches apart.

Bake 8 to 10 minutes, until puffy and tops begin to crack. Cool on cookie sheets 2 minutes. Transfer cookies, still on parchment, to wire racks to cool completely.

In a small saucepan, heat cream until it simmers slightly. Remove from heat, and whisk in chopped chocolate and vanilla. Stir until smooth.

Add coconut. Stir until combined. Cool 40 to 45 minutes at room temperature, stirring occasionally, until filling mixture begins to thicken.

Spread 1 tsp. filling over flat side of a cookie. Place a second cookie, flat side down, on top of the filling, and gently press cookies together. Repeat with remaining cookies.

Store unfilled cookies in an airtight container, at room temperature, for up to 5 days.

INGREDIENTS

¾ cup all-purpose flour
¼ cup Dutch-process cocoa
¼ tsp. baking soda
¼ tsp. sweet curry powder
⅛ tsp. ground cardamom
⅛ tsp. fine sea salt
6 tbsp. (¾ stick) unsalted butter, room temperature
¼ cup granulated sugar
¼ cup packed light brown sugar
1 tsp. pure vanilla extract
1 large egg yolk, room temperature

Filling
3 tbsp. heavy cream
2 oz. bittersweet or semisweet chocolate, finely chopped
⅛ tsp. pure vanilla extract
3 tbsp. finely chopped, unsweetened coconut

Glazed Bittersweet Chocolate Sablés
Makes 36 to 42 cookies

For more than a year, I experimented with different combinations of chocolate and orange ingredients. I found that this rich chocolate sablé, iced with orange glaze, is the perfect balance of chocolate and orange. If you are not an orange fan, simply dust cooled cookies with powdered sugar, for an equally delicious treat.

In a medium bowl, sift together flour, baking powder, sea salt, and cocoa. Whisk in almond flour.

In the large bowl of an electric mixer, with speed set to high, beat butter and sugar, about 2 minutes, until pale and fluffy. Add the egg yolk and vanilla. Beat until combined.

Set speed to low, and add the flour mixture. Mix until combined. Add the chocolate. Mix until combined. Place in covered bowl, and chill for 30 minutes, until firm.

Preheat oven to 350 degrees. Line cookie sheets with parchment paper.

Using a small cookie scoop (#100), shape dough into 1-inch balls and drop onto prepared cookie sheets, spacing them about 2 inches apart. Using the bottom of a glass or back of a spoon, flatten each to ⅓-inch thickness. Bake 10 to 12 minutes, until firm to the touch. Transfer cookies, still on parchment, to wire racks to cool completely.

In a small mixing bowl, mix powdered sugar, orange oil, and water until smooth and thoroughly combined. Brush cooled cookies with glaze. Garnish each cookie with a small piece of candied orange peel, if desired. Alternatively, dust cooled cookies with powdered sugar.

Store in an airtight container, at room temperature, for 3 to 5 days.

INGREDIENTS

- 1 cup all-purpose flour
- ¼ tsp. baking powder
- ¼ tsp. fine sea salt
- 2½ tbsp. Dutch-process cocoa
- 2½ tbsp. almond flour
- 8 tbsp. (1 stick) unsalted butter, room temperature
- ¼ cup granulated sugar
- 1 large egg yolk, room temperature
- 1 tsp. pure vanilla extract
- 3 oz. bittersweet or semisweet chocolate, finely chopped

Glaze
- ½ cup powdered sugar, sifted
- ⅛ tsp. orange oil (or substitute ¼ tsp. pure orange extract plus ¼ tsp. grated orange zest, packed)
- 1½ tbsp. boiling water
- ½ tsp. finely chopped candied orange peel (optional)

Vanilla-Dusted Chocolate Drops
Makes 30 to 36 cookies

Chocolate shortbread cookies are a staple in my household. Adding chocolate chips and a vanilla sugar dusting deepens their chocolate flavor. If you don't want to make your own vanilla sugar, you can find premixed packets at specialty baking stores or online.

In a medium bowl, sift together flour, cocoa, and espresso powder. (If using vanilla extract instead of espresso powder, add as directed below.) Whisk in sugar.

Using a pastry cutter, cut in butter until dough resembles flakes. If using vanilla extract instead of espresso powder, stir in, until completely dispersed throughout dough. Stir in chocolate chips.

Knead with hands until gathered together, smooth, and pliable. Place dough in a covered bowl, and chill for 45 minutes to 1 hour, until firm.

To prepare topping, place sugar and vanilla bean pieces in a small food processor bowl. Pulse until vanilla bean is pulverized. Pass sugar mixture through a fine sieve to remove seeds. Discard seeds. Set topping aside.

Preheat oven to 350 degrees. Line cookie sheets with parchment paper.

Using a small cookie scoop (#100), shape dough into 1-inch balls and drop onto prepared cookie sheets, spacing them about 2 inches apart. Bake 14 to 15 minutes, until slightly firm to the touch. Cool on cookie sheets for 2 minutes.

Transfer cookies, still on parchment, to wire racks. While cookies are still warm, dust with vanilla sugar. Cool completely.

Store in an airtight container, at room temperature, for up to 3 days.

INGREDIENTS

1 cup all-purpose flour
2 tbsp. Dutch-process cocoa
¼ tsp. instant espresso powder (or substitute ½ tsp. pure vanilla extract)
¼ cup granulated sugar
8 tbsp. (1 stick) cold butter, cut into ½-inch cubes
⅓ cup mini semisweet chocolate chips

Topping
½ cup granulated sugar
½ vanilla bean, cut into 2 pieces

Baker's Note: Store any unused vanilla sugar in an airtight container, at room temperature, for future use.

Not Your Mother's Bar Cookies

It wasn't until I was an adult that I really started to enjoy brownies, blondies, and other bar cookies. That was because I started to experiment with flavors to make these traditionally sweet cookies a bit more edgy and grownup. This chapter features some of my own special favorites, such as goat cheese brownies, polenta blondies, and gluten-free mango-coconut bars.

Goat Cheese and Caramel-Swirl Brownies
Makes 20 to 24 brownies

These delicious chocolate brownies, with tangy goat cheese and dulce de leche, are a unique dessert choice. If you have Mexican vanilla, use it in this recipe wherever vanilla extract is specified.

Preheat oven to 350 degrees. Line the sides and bottom of an 8x8-inch baking pan with foil, leaving an overhang of about 2 inches on each of 2 opposite sides. Cut parchment paper to fit bottom of pan, and place on foil. Lightly grease pan sides with oil.

In a medium bowl, sift together flour, baking powder, and salt. Set aside.

In the top of a double boiler, set over gently simmering water, melt chocolates and butter. Stir constantly until fully combined and smooth. Remove from heat.

Add sugar and vanilla to chocolate mixture. Mix thoroughly. Cool about 5 minutes. Whisk in eggs, one at a time. Gradually whisk flour mixture into chocolate mixture, until fully incorporated.

In the small bowl of an electric mixer, combine the filling ingredients. Set speed to high and cream for 1 to 2 minutes, until light and fluffy.

In a medium bowl, combine the topping ingredients. Mix until smooth and thoroughly combined.

Pour half of the brownie mixture into the prepared pan. Smooth top. Spoon half of the goat cheese filling onto the batter, in dollops.

Pour remaining brownie mixture over the filling. Spoon dulce de leche topping onto the batter, in dollops. Spoon remaining goat cheese filling onto the batter, in dollops. With a knife, carefully swirl to create a marble pattern. Do not overmix.

Bake 50 to 60 minutes, until center is raised and firm to the touch. Sides will pull away from pan slightly. Cool completely in pan, placed on a wire rack. Using foil overhang as an aid, lift uncut brownies out of pan. Cut just prior to serving.

Store in an airtight container, at room temperature, for up to 3 days.

INGREDIENTS

⅔ cup all-purpose flour
½ tsp. baking powder
¼ tsp. salt
3 oz. unsweetened chocolate
3 oz. bittersweet chocolate
6 tbsp. (¾ stick) unsalted butter
1 cup granulated sugar
2 tsp. pure vanilla extract
3 large eggs, room temperature

Filling
1 cup (about 6.5 oz.) plain goat cheese
2½ tbsp. granulated sugar
¼ tsp. pure vanilla extract
1 large egg yolk, room temperature

Topping
1 cup canned dulce de leche
1 tsp. pure vanilla extract
2 tbsp. boiling water

Cardamom-Ginger Bars
Makes 20 to 24 bars

Fresh ginger and fragrant cardamom infuse these tender, moist, cakelike bar cookies with a heavenly taste and aroma. After one bite, they will be your new favorite. These are great as a breakfast cookie or with a dollop of whipped cream as a dessert.

Preheat oven to 350 degrees. Line the sides and bottom of a 9x13-inch baking pan with foil, leaving an overhang of about 2 inches on each of 2 opposite sides. Cut parchment paper to fit bottom of pan, and place on foil. Lightly butter parchment. Set aside.

In a medium bowl, sift together flour, baking powder, cardamom, ground ginger, and sea salt. Set aside.

In the large bowl of an electric mixer, with speed set to high, beat butter and sugar 2 to 3 minutes, until pale and fluffy. Add eggs, vanilla, orange zest, and fresh ginger. Beat about 2 minutes until incorporated.

Reduce speed to low. Mix in flour mixture until incorporated. Mix in apple, walnuts, and optional crystallized ginger.

Pour batter into prepared pan. Smooth top. Bake 30 to 35 minutes, until top is golden brown and firm to the touch. Cool completely in pan. Using foil overhang as an aid, lift uncut cookies out of pan, and cut into bars.

Store in an airtight container, at room temperature, for up to 5 days.

INGREDIENTS

- 1⅔ cups all-purpose flour
- 1 tsp. baking powder
- 1 tsp. ground cardamom
- ¾ tsp. ground ginger
- ¾ tsp. sea salt
- 8 tbsp. (1 stick) unsalted butter, room temperature
- 1 cup packed light brown sugar
- 3 large eggs, room temperature
- 1 tsp. pure vanilla extract
- 2 tsp. grated orange zest, packed
- 1 tbsp. grated fresh ginger with juices, packed
- ½ cup diced Granny Smith or other tart apple
- ¾ cup coarsely chopped walnuts
- 1½ tbsp. finely chopped crystallized ginger (optional)

Lemon Yogurt Squares
Makes 16 bars

The light and tangy, lemony yogurt filling of these squares pairs perfectly with their toasted hazelnut crust. They are a great alternative to cheesecake bars.

Preheat oven to 350 degrees. Line the sides and bottom of an 8x8-inch baking pan with foil, leaving an overhang of about 2 inches on each of 2 opposite sides. Cut parchment paper to fit bottom of pan, and place on foil.

Melt butter in small saucepan over low heat, and cool slightly.

Place flour, sugar, hazelnuts, and salt in a food processor. Pulse until nuts are finely ground. Add melted butter and vanilla. Pulse until mixture begins to clump.

Remove dough, and gather together. Press dough evenly over the bottom of the pan. Smooth top. Bake about 18 to 20 minutes, until light brown.

While crust is baking, prepare filling. In the large bowl of an electric mixer, combine eggs and sugar. Set mixer speed to high, and beat 2 to 3 minutes, until mixture is light and fluffy.

Add yogurt, lemon juice, and lemon zest. Beat about 1 minute, until combined. Set mixer to low. Add flour. Mix until combined.

Remove crust from oven and gently pour filling over hot crust. Smooth top and return to oven. Bake 35 to 40 minutes, until filling sets. Top will be cracked, and edges will be golden brown. Cool completely in pan, placed on a wire rack. Using foil overhang as an aid, lift uncut cookies out of pan, and cut into 16 squares.

Store in an airtight container, in the refrigerator, for up to 3 days.

INGREDIENTS

8 tbsp. (1 stick) unsalted butter
¾ cup all-purpose flour
¼ cup granulated sugar
¼ cup toasted hazelnuts
⅛ tsp. salt
½ tsp. pure vanilla extract

Filling
2 large eggs, room temperature
½ cup granulated sugar
1¼ cups (about 14 oz.) Greek whole-fat
   yogurt, room temperature
2 tbsp. fresh lemon juice
2 tsp. grated lemon zest, packed
2 tbsp. all-purpose flour

Gingerbread and Pumpkin Brownies
Makes 20 brownies

Enjoyed along with a cup of hot coffee or tea, these are the perfect moist treat on a crisp autumn afternoon.

Preheat oven to 350 degrees. Line the sides and bottom of a 9x13-inch baking pan with foil, leaving an overhang of about 2 inches on each of 2 opposite sides. Cut parchment paper to fit bottom of pan, and place on foil. Lightly butter parchment. Set aside.

In a medium bowl, sift together flour, baking powder, salt, and spices. Set aside.

In the top of a double boiler, set over gently simmering water, melt butter and chocolate. Stir constantly until fully combined and mixture is smooth. Remove from heat. Cool about 5 minutes.

To chocolate mixture, add brown sugar, molasses, and vanilla. Mix thoroughly until smooth. Whisk in eggs, one at a time. Whisk flour mixture, in thirds, into chocolate mixture, until fully incorporated.

In a medium bowl, combine filling ingredients. Mix thoroughly. Set aside.

Pour half of the brownie mixture into the prepared pan. Smooth top. Spoon pumpkin filling onto the batter, in dollops.

Pour remaining brownie mixture over pumpkin filling. With a knife, carefully swirl to create a marble pattern. Do not overmix.

Bake 40 to 45 minutes, until center is raised and firm to the touch. Sides will pull away from pan slightly. Cool completely in pan, placed on a wire rack. Using foil overhang as an aid, lift uncut brownies out of pan, and cut into 20 bars.

Store in an airtight container, at room temperature, for up to 5 days.

INGREDIENTS

2 cups all-purpose flour
1 tsp. baking powder
½ tsp. salt
2 tsp. ground ginger
1½ tsp. ground cinnamon
¼ tsp. ground cloves
8 tbsp. (1 stick) unsalted butter
6 oz. bittersweet chocolate, chopped
1 cup packed dark brown sugar
½ cup dark molasses
2 tsp. pure vanilla extract
4 large eggs, room temperature

Filling
1 cup solid-pack pureed pumpkin
3 tbsp. heavy cream
¼ tsp. ground cardamom
¼ tsp. ground nutmeg

Baker's Note: For a slightly sweeter brownie, substitute semisweet chocolate for the bittersweet chocolate.

Polenta Blondies
Makes 16 bars

Everyone will love these not-too-sweet, chewy cornmeal blondies, packed with almonds and pears. If you can't find dried pears, substitute dried apples or dried apricots.

Preheat oven to 350 degrees. Line the sides and bottom of an 8x8-inch baking pan with foil, leaving an overhang of about 2 inches on each of 2 opposite sides. Cut parchment paper to fit bottom of pan, and place on foil. Lightly butter parchment. Set aside.

In a medium bowl, sift together flour, cornmeal, and salt. Set aside.

Melt butter in small saucepan, over low heat, and cool 2 minutes.

In the large bowl of an electric mixer, with speed set to high, beat melted butter and sugars, about 2 minutes, until smooth. Add egg, vanilla, and almond extract. Beat about 2 minutes, until fluffy.

Reduce speed to low. Mix in flour mixture until combined. Mix in dried pears and almonds.

Pour batter into prepared pan. Smooth top. Bake 30 to 40 minutes, until top is golden brown and firm to the touch. Sides will pull away from pan, and top will be slightly cracked. Cool completely in pan, placed on wire rack. Using foil overhang as an aid, lift uncut blondies out of pan, and cut into 16 bars.

Store in an airtight container, at room temperature, for up to 5 days.

INGREDIENTS

½ cup all-purpose flour
½ cup finely ground yellow cornmeal
$\frac{1}{16}$ tsp. salt
8 tbsp. (1 stick) unsalted butter
½ cup packed dark brown sugar
½ cup granulated sugar
1 large egg, room temperature
1 tsp. pure vanilla extract
½ tsp. pure almond extract
⅓ cup diced dried pears
⅔ cup chopped, lightly toasted whole almonds (see Baker's Note)

Baker's Note: Lightly toast whole almonds at 350 degrees, 8 to 10 minutes, to bring out their flavor.

Mango-Coconut Bars
Makes 20 to 24 bars, *gluten-free*

Coconut-chocolate candies from Anastasia Confections were the inspiration for this tropical, gluten-free bar. Mango puree is combined with sweet coconut and accented by lime and chocolate, making a truly decadent treat.

Preheat oven to 325 degrees. Line the sides and bottom of a 9x13-inch baking pan with foil, leaving an overhang of about 2 inches on each of 2 opposite sides. Cut parchment paper to fit bottom of pan, and place on foil.

In the top of a double boiler, set over gently simmering water, melt the chocolate. Spread the melted chocolate evenly in the bottom of the pan. Smooth top. Refrigerate until set, at least 10 minutes.

While chocolate is chilling, prepare the filling. In a medium saucepan, over low heat, stir together mango puree and sugar. Heat about 1 minute, stirring until sugar dissolves and mixture is smooth (mixture should not come to a boil).

Remove from heat. Cool about 5 minutes, stirring constantly. Stir in condensed milk, sweetened and unsweetened coconut, and lime zest. Add lightly beaten egg whites, and mix until evenly moist throughout.

Spread filling evenly over hardened chocolate. Smooth top. Bake 50 to 55 minutes, until top is golden brown.

Cool completely in pan, placed on wire rack. Then refrigerate at least 2 hours, until chocolate base is firm. Using foil overhang as an aid, lift uncut cookies out of pan, and cut into 20 to 24 bars.

Store in an airtight container, in the refrigerator, for up to 2 weeks.

INGREDIENTS

8 oz. semisweet chocolate, chopped

Filling
1 cup mango puree, room temperature
1 cup granulated sugar
1⅓ cups (about 14 oz.) sweetened condensed milk
2 cups sweetened coconut, finely chopped
1 cup unsweetened coconut, finely chopped
1 tbsp. grated lime zest, packed
2 large egg whites, room temperature, lightly beaten

Baker's Note: To make your own mango puree, place about 2 cups fresh or thawed mango fruit chunks in a food processor, and blend until smooth.

Blueberry-Almond Squares
Makes 16 bars

These blueberry bars look like a cobbler with a light almond-egg-white topping. They are sweet and tender and pack a powerful blueberry taste. Use dried wild blueberries for best results.

Preheat oven to 350 degrees. Line the sides and bottom of an 8x8-inch baking pan with foil, leaving an overhang of about 2 inches on each of 2 opposite sides. Cut parchment paper to fit bottom of pan, and place on foil.

In a medium bowl, sift together the flour and salt. Set aside.

In the large bowl of an electric mixer, combine butter, sugar, and vanilla. Set mixer speed to high and beat 1 to 2 minutes, until light and fluffy. Reduce mixer speed to low. Add flour mixture, and mix until combined.

Press dough evenly into the bottom of prepared pan. With a fork, pierce entire surface of dough. Bake 12 to 15 minutes, until puffy and beginning to set.

While crust is baking, prepare topping. In the large bowl of a food processor, pulse almond flour, egg whites, sugar, and almond extract until well blended. Set aside.

As soon as crust comes out of the oven, sprinkle dried blueberries evenly over crust. Pour almond-egg-white mixture evenly over crust. Sprinkle with finely chopped almonds. Press almonds down lightly.

Return pan to oven and bake 20 to 25 minutes, until topping is puffy and golden. Cool completely in pan, placed on a wire rack. Using foil overhang as an aid, lift uncut cookies out of pan, and cut into 16 squares.

Store in an airtight container, at room temperature, for up to 3 days.

INGREDIENTS

1 cup all-purpose flour
¼ tsp. salt
8 tbsp. (1 stick) unsalted butter, room temperature
½ cup granulated sugar
½ tsp. pure vanilla extract

Topping
⅔ cup almond flour
2 large egg whites, room temperature
½ cup granulated sugar
½ tsp. pure almond extract
⅔ cup dried blueberries
3 tbsp. finely chopped blanched almonds

Nutty, Fruity Treats

Fruits such as oranges, limes, and figs, and nuts such as walnuts, pistachios, and cashews, impart sophistication to these cookies, which were inspired by Asian, European, and Latin American flavors.

Walnut Sablés with Orange-Honey Filling
Makes 60 to 72 unfilled cookies or 30 to 36 sandwich cookies

The fresh orange zest and honey filling nicely complements the toasty walnuts in these tender sablé cookies. Once you taste them, you will become a fan. These cookies are also delicious served unfilled.

Preheat oven to 350 degrees. Line cookie sheets with parchment paper.

In a medium bowl, sift together flour and salt. Set aside.

In the large bowl of an electric mixer, with speed set to medium, cream butter, sugar, and vanilla, 2 to 3 minutes, until light and fluffy. Set speed to low, and mix in flour until combined. Add walnuts, and mix until combined. Gather dough together, and shape into disk.

Roll out dough, between 2 sheets of wax paper, to ¼-inch thickness. Using a 1- to 1½-inch round cookie cutter, cut out cookies. Transfer cookies to prepared cookie sheets, spacing 1 inch apart.

Sprinkle half with raw sugar. Bake 10 to 12 minutes, until light golden brown. Transfer cookies, still on parchment, to wire racks to cool completely.

In the small bowl of an electric mixer, with speed set to high, beat butter and powdered sugar 2 to 3 minutes, until light and fluffy. Add honey. Beat about 1 minute to combine.

Add orange zest to filling, and beat 1 to 2 minutes, until smooth and creamy. Transfer to a small bowl. Use immediately or cover and refrigerate. Return to room temperature before serving.

Just before serving, spread ½ tsp. filling onto flat side of a plain cookie. Place a sugared cookie, flat side down, on top of filling and gently press cookies together. Repeat with remaining cookies.

Store unfilled cookies in an airtight container, at room temperature, for up to 5 days.

INGREDIENTS

1 cup all-purpose flour
⅛ tsp. salt
8 tbsp. (1 stick) unsalted butter, room temperature
½ cup granulated sugar
½ tsp. pure vanilla extract
½ cup finely chopped toasted walnuts (see Baker's Note)
Raw sugar, such as demerara, for sprinkling

Filling
4 tbsp. (½ stick) unsalted butter, room temperature
1 cup powdered sugar
½ tbsp. honey
2 tsp. grated orange zest, packed

Baker's Note: Toast walnuts at 350 degrees, 6 to 7 minutes, to bring out their flavor.

Anise-Scented Pistachio Cookies
Makes 36 to 40 cookies

Pistachios give these delicious cookies a crispy, crumbly texture, and the hint of anise takes dessert into new territory. Needless to say, these are one of my favorites.

Preheat oven to 350 degrees. Line cookie sheets with parchment paper.

In a medium bowl, sift together flour, baking powder, and salt. Set aside.

In the large bowl of an electric mixer, with speed set to medium, beat butter 1 to 2 minutes, until creamy. Gradually add sugar. Mix well.

Add egg yolk, and beat 1 to 2 minutes, until well combined. Add lemon zest and extracts, and mix until well combined. Set mixer speed to low. Gradually add flour mixture. Mix until well combined.

Add pistachios. Mix until combined. Dough will be crumbly. Knead dough by hand and gather together.

Using a small cookie scoop (#100), shape dough into 1-inch balls and drop onto prepared cookie sheets, spacing them 2 inches apart. Flatten balls slightly with bottom of a glass or back of a spoon. Sprinkle with additional chopped pistachios.

Bake 12 to 14 minutes, until light golden brown on the bottom and edges. Cool 5 minutes on cookie sheets. Transfer cookies, still on parchment, to wire racks to cool completely.

Store in an airtight container, at room temperature, for up to 1 week.

INGREDIENTS

1 cup all-purpose flour
½ tsp. baking powder
¼ tsp. salt
8 tbsp. (1 stick) unsalted butter, room temperature
¾ cup granulated sugar
1 large egg yolk, room temperature
2 tsp. grated lemon zest, packed
1 tsp. pure almond extract
¼ tsp. anise extract
¼ cup plus 2 tbsp. chopped, unsalted shelled pistachios, plus additional 3 tbsp. chopped pistachios for sprinkling

Flourless Peanut Butter Cookies Noir
Makes 18 to 24 cookies, *gluten-free*

My fondness for sesame seeds sent me on a quest for the perfect cookie pairing. The tender peanut butter base of these cookies nicely complements the crunchy, nutty sesame seeds on top. Black sesame seeds make a very attractive presentation, but if you cannot find them, white sesame seeds can be substituted without much difference in flavor.

Preheat oven to 350 degrees. Line cookie sheets with parchment paper.

In a large bowl, whisk together sugar, baking soda, and sea salt. Add peanut butter and beaten egg. Stir with a large spoon until combined.

Using a medium cookie scoop (#40), shape dough into 1½-inch balls. Dip tops in sesame seeds. Place balls on prepared cookie sheets 2 inches apart.

Bake 12 to 13 minutes, until puffed and cracked. Cool on cookie sheets for 2 minutes. Transfer cookies, still on parchment, to wire racks to cool completely.

Store in an airtight container, at room temperature, for up to 1 week.

INGREDIENTS
¾ cup granulated sugar
½ tsp. baking soda
¼ tsp. fine sea salt
1 cup unsalted, creamy, organic peanut butter, room temperature
1 large egg, room temperature, lightly beaten
5 tbsp. black sesame seeds

Lime Butter Cookies
Makes 18 to 24 cookies

I love lime. And I especially love lime cookies. These 2½-inch cookies were inspired by polvorones, *the buttery cookies found in a variety of citrus and fruit flavors in Latino bakeries. I use Boyajian lime oil in my cookies (www. boyajianinc.com).*

In a medium bowl, sift together flour, baking powder, and baking soda. Whisk in milk powder. Set aside.

In the large bowl of an electric mixer, with speed set to high, cream butter, shortening, and sugar, about 2 minutes, until light and fluffy. Add lime juice, lime zest, lime oil, and egg. Beat 2 to 3 minutes, until incorporated.

Reduce mixer speed to low. Gradually add flour mixture. Mix until well combined and dough is smooth. Put dough in covered bowl, and refrigerate 1 to 2 hours, or overnight, for flavors to develop.

Preheat oven to 350 degrees. Line cookie sheets with parchment paper.

Using a medium cookie scoop (#40), drop 1½-inch balls on prepared sheets, spacing 2½ inches apart. Cookies will spread considerably during baking, so allow adequate space. With the bottom of a glass or back of a spoon, flatten the balls to ⅓-inch thickness.

Sprinkle with colored sanding sugar or granulated sugar. Bake 12 to 14 minutes, until cookies puff in the center and edges are brown. Transfer cookies, still on parchment, to wire racks to cool completely.

Store in an airtight container, at room temperature, for up to 3 days.

INGREDIENTS

1 cup all-purpose flour
½ tsp. baking powder
⅛ tsp. baking soda
1 tbsp. nonfat dry milk powder
4 tbsp. (½ stick) unsalted butter, room temperature
2 tbsp. vegetable shortening, room temperature
½ cup granulated sugar
1 tbsp. fresh lime juice
½ tsp. grated lime zest, packed
¼ tsp. lime oil
1 large egg, room temperature
Light green sanding sugar or granulated sugar for sprinkling

Pecan Shortbread and
Dulce de Leche Sandwich Cookies
Makes 60 to 64 unfilled cookies or 30 to 32 sandwich cookies

Dulce de leche is one of my weaknesses. So are buttery, sandy, pecan shortbread cookies. Hence, beware! *This petite pecan shortbread variation on South American alfajores is absolutely addictive.*

In a medium bowl, sift together flour, baking powder, and salt. Set aside.

In the large bowl of an electric mixer, with speed set to high, cream butter and sugar 1 to 2 minutes, until smooth. Add pecans and vanilla. Mix 1 to 2 minutes, until thoroughly combined.

Reduce speed to low. Add flour mixture, and mix until just combined and crumbly. Gather dough together with hands and shape into disk about ½-inch thick. Refrigerate 2 hours, or overnight, until firm.

Preheat oven to 350 degrees. Line cookie sheets with parchment paper.

Roll out dough, between 2 sheets of wax paper, to ¼-inch thickness, and cut with a 1-inch round cookie cutter. Place on prepared sheets, spacing 1 inch apart. Bake 8 to 10 minutes, until light golden brown. Cool on cookie sheets for 1 minute. Transfer cookies, still on parchment, to wire racks to cool completely.

In a small bowl, mix dulce de leche and vanilla until well combined. Just before serving, spread ½ tsp. filling onto flat side of a cookie. Place a second cookie, flat side down, on top of filling and gently press cookies together. Repeat with remaining cookies. Lightly dust the top of each cookie with powdered sugar.

Store unfilled cookies in an airtight container, at room temperature, for up to 5 days.

INGREDIENTS

1 cup all-purpose flour
½ tsp. baking powder
¼ tsp. salt
8 tbsp. (1 stick) unsalted butter, room temperature
⅓ cup granulated sugar
½ cup finely ground toasted pecans (see Baker's Note)
1 tsp. pure vanilla extract
3 tbsp. powdered sugar for dusting, sifted

Filling
¾ cup canned dulce de leche
½ tsp. pure vanilla extract

Baker's Note: Toast pecans at 350 degrees for 5 minutes, to bring out their full flavor.

Black Mission Fig Cookies
Makes 40 to 48 cookies

I originally used fresh figs in this not-too-sweet, soft cookie. But given the limited June-to-October season for figs, I modified the recipe for dried figs, so I could enjoy these cookies year round. Black Mission figs, which are smaller and sweeter than Calimyrna figs, are especially good in this delicious treat, but either works well.

Preheat oven to 350 degrees. Line cookie sheets with parchment paper.

In a medium bowl, sift together pastry flour, baking soda, baking powder, salt, and five-spice powder. Set aside.

Place walnuts in food processor and grind until fine. Take care not to overgrind and turn nuts into nut butter. Whisk ground nuts into pastry flour mixture.

In the large bowl of an electric mixer, with speed set to high, beat butter and maple syrup 2 to 3 minutes, until light and fluffy. Add egg and vanilla. Beat about 2 minutes until combined.

Add ground figs. Mix until figs are distributed throughout dough. Reduce speed to low, and gradually add flour mixture until incorporated. Dough will be soft.

Using a medium cookie scoop (#40), place 1½-inch balls on prepared sheets, spacing 2 inches apart. Bake 12 to 14 minutes, until golden brown and firm to the touch. Cool completely on cookie sheets.

Store in an airtight container, at room temperature, for up to 3 days.

INGREDIENTS

1 cup whole-wheat pastry flour
½ tsp. baking soda
¼ tsp. baking powder
¼ tsp. salt
¼ tsp. Chinese five-spice powder
1 cup toasted walnuts
8 tbsp. (1 stick) unsalted butter, room temperature
¼ cup maple syrup
1 large egg, room temperature
½ tsp. pure vanilla extract
1 cup ground, dried Black Mission figs

Baker's Note: If you do not have whole-wheat pastry flour, all-purpose flour can be substituted. A food processor can be used to grind the figs.

Apricot-Cherry Shortbread
Makes 30 to 36 cookies

My friend Ankit is a fiend for apricots. I made these for him. I added the cherries for myself.

In a medium bowl, sift together flour and sea salt. Whisk in sugar.

With a pastry cutter, cut in butter until it resembles flakes. With a fork, stir in extracts and disperse throughout dough. Stir in dried fruit. Knead dough with hands, until gathered together and pliable.

Roll into a 1½-inch by 9-inch log. Wrap log in wax paper or plastic wrap, and chill for at least 2 hours, or overnight.

Preheat oven to 350 degrees. Line cookie sheets with parchment paper.

Slice log into ¼-inch-thick slices, place on prepared sheets 2 inches apart, and sprinkle with sugar, if desired. Bake 12 to 15 minutes, until pale golden brown. Cool on cookie sheets for 2 minutes. Transfer cookies, still on parchment, to wire racks to cool completely.

Store in an airtight container, at room temperature, for up to 5 days.

INGREDIENTS

1 cup all-purpose flour
⅛ tsp. fine sea salt
¼ cup granulated sugar
8 tbsp. (1 stick) cold butter, cut into ½-inch cubes
¼ tsp. pure vanilla extract
¼ tsp. pure almond extract
2 tbsp. finely chopped dried apricots
2 tbsp. finely chopped dried cherries
3 tbsp. coarse sanding sugar or raw sugar, such as demerara, for sprinkling (optional)

Fleur de Sel Cashew Cookies
Makes 18 to 24 cookies, *gluten-free*

Organic cashew butter and roasted, unsalted cashews make these dense cookies a great alternative to peanut butter cookies. Finish them with fine or coarse fleur de sel sea salt for a sophisticated twist. If you cannot find it, you can substitute another type of delicately flavored sea salt, such as Himalayan pink or Mediterranean.

Preheat oven to 350 degrees. Line cookie sheets with parchment paper.

In a large bowl, whisk together sugar, baking soda, and sea salt. Add cashew butter and beaten egg. Stir with a large spoon until combined. Stir in chopped cashews. The dough will be a little crumbly.

Using a medium cookie scoop (#40), drop 1½-inch balls on prepared sheets, spacing 2 inches apart. With the bottom of a glass or back of a spoon, flatten the balls to ½-inch thickness.

Bake 12 to 15 minutes, until golden brown. If desired, sprinkle each cookie with a few grains of sea salt. Cool completely on cookie sheets.

Store in an airtight container, at room temperature, for up to 1 week.

INGREDIENTS

¾ cup granulated sugar
½ tsp. baking soda
¼ tsp. fine fleur de sel or other fine sea salt
1 cup unsalted, creamy, organic cashew butter, room temperature
1 large egg, room temperature, beaten to 3 times volume
½ cup chopped unsalted, roasted cashews
Fine or coarse fleur de sel or other sea salt for sprinkling (optional)

Herby, Cheesy Savories

Herbs, cheese, and even bacon make an appearance in these fun treats that challenge the traditional territory of sweet cookies. After all, cookies shouldn't just be limited to dessert. They can be cocktail-party appetizers as well as savory accompaniments to soup or salad.

Rosemary-Cornmeal Butter Cookies
Makes 18 to 24 cookies

These light cookies, packed with fragrant rosemary, are delicious on their own or as an accompaniment to an assortment of after-dinner cheeses. If you want them bite-size, use a small scoop, such as #100, and shorten the baking time by 1 or 2 minutes.

Preheat oven to 350 degrees. Line cookie sheets with parchment paper.

In a medium bowl, sift together flour, cornmeal, cream of tartar, baking soda, and salt. Set aside.

In the large bowl of an electric mixer, with speed set to high, cream together butter and granulated sugar, about 1 minute. Add the egg yolk, and mix until smooth. Mix in rosemary until completely dispersed throughout dough.

Set mixer speed to low, and add flour mixture until just incorporated. Dough will be a little crumbly. Knead with hands, and gather together.

Using a medium cookie scoop (#60), shape dough into 1¼-inch balls. Dip the top of each ball into raw sugar. Space cookies 2 inches apart on prepared cookie sheets. Using the bottom of a glass or back of a spoon, flatten the balls to ⅓-inch thickness. Bake 10 to 12 minutes, until cookies are slightly browned on the edges. Transfer cookies, still on parchment, to wire racks to cool completely.

Store in an airtight container, at room temperature, for up to 5 days.

INGREDIENTS

¾ cup all-purpose flour
¼ cup finely ground yellow cornmeal
½ tsp. cream of tartar
½ tsp. baking soda
⅛ tsp. salt
6 tbsp. (¾ stick) unsalted butter, room temperature
½ cup granulated sugar
1 large egg yolk, room temperature
1 tbsp. finely chopped, fresh rosemary
Raw sugar, such as demerara

Baker's Note: Using a #100 scoop will make 30 to 36 cookies.

Blue Cheese and Cranberry Cookies
Makes 48 to 54 cookies

These light cookies, with tangy blue cheese and tart cranberries, are a perfect after-dinner treat. The sugar sprinkled on top heightens the fruity cranberry accents and balances the savory cheese flavor. I make these cookies with pecans, but walnuts can be substituted.

In a medium bowl, sift together flour, cornstarch, and sea salt. Set aside.

In the large bowl of an electric mixer, with speed set to high, cream together blue cheese and butter. Add sugar, and beat about 2 minutes, until light and fluffy. Reduce mixer speed to low and add flour mixture. Mix until just combined.

Add cranberries and pecans. Mix until evenly distributed throughout dough. Dough will be crumbly. With hands, knead dough until soft and pliable.

Divide dough into 2 pieces and roll each piece into a 1-inch by 9-inch log. Wrap logs in wax paper or plastic wrap. Refrigerate until firm, at least 2 hours, or overnight.

Preheat oven to 350 degrees. Line cookie sheets with parchment paper.

Slice 1 log into ¼-inch-thick slices, place on prepared sheets 1 inch apart, and sprinkle with sugar. Bake 12 to 14 minutes, until bottoms begin to brown and tops just begin to turn golden. Transfer cookies, still on parchment, to wire racks to cool completely. Repeat with second log.

Store in an airtight container, at room temperature, for up to 5 days.

INGREDIENTS

1¼ cups all-purpose flour
½ cup cornstarch
¼ tsp. fine sea salt
1 scant cup (about 4 oz.) domestic blue cheese, room temperature
10 tbsp. (1¼ sticks) unsalted butter, room temperature
¼ cup granulated sugar
⅓ cup dried cranberries, finely chopped
⅔ cup chopped pecans
Coarse sanding sugar or raw sugar, such as demerara, for sprinkling

Parmesan Cheese Coins with Mascarpone Filling
Makes 60 to 72 unfilled cookies or 30 to 36 sandwich cookies

Filled with a savory basil-tomato-mascarpone cheese, these light and cheesy shortbread-style cookies are like a taste of spring. They are terrific as an appetizer or served as a fancy cocktail-party cookie.

In a medium bowl, sift together flour, baking soda, and sea salt. Whisk in almond flour. Set aside.

In the large bowl of an electric mixer, with speed set to high, cream butter, 1 to 2 minutes. Add cheese, and beat about 1 minute, until fluffy. Add egg, and beat 1 to 2 minutes, until light and fluffy. Reduce mixer speed to low, and add flour mixture. Mix until just combined.

Divide dough into 2 disks. Wrap disks in wax paper or plastic wrap, and refrigerate until firm, at least 30 minutes.

Preheat oven to 350 degrees. Line cookie sheets with parchment paper.

Roll out dough, between 2 sheets of wax paper, to ¼-inch thickness. Using a 1- to 1½-inch round cookie cutter, cut out cookies. Transfer cookies to prepared sheets, spacing 1 inch apart. Bake 10 to 12 minutes, until bottoms begin to brown and tops begin to turn golden. Transfer cookies, still on parchment, to wire racks to cool completely.

In a small bowl, combine filling ingredients, and mix until creamy. Cover and refrigerate for 30 minutes, for flavors to meld.

Prior to serving, return filling to room temperature. On the flat side of a cookie, spread ½ tsp. filling. Place a second cookie, flat side down, on top of filling and gently press cookies together. Repeat with remaining cookies.

Store unfilled cookies in an airtight container, at room temperature, for up to 5 days.

INGREDIENTS

1 cup all-purpose flour
¼ tsp. baking soda
¼ tsp. sea salt
¼ cup almond flour
8 tbsp. (1 stick) unsalted butter, room temperature
⅔ cup freshly grated parmesan or parmesan-Romano cheese
1 large egg, room temperature

Filling
½ cup (about 4 oz.) mascarpone cheese
2 tbsp. finely chopped, fresh basil leaves, packed
2 tbsp. finely chopped sundried tomatoes
¼ tsp. freshly ground black pepper

Baker's Note: As an alternative, make filled thumbprint cookies. Using a #60 scoop, drop dough onto cookie sheets, make a thumbprint depression in the center of each cookie, and bake. After cooling, fill the thumbprint depression with mascarpone filling.

Black Olive Bites
Makes 18 to 24 cookies

Earthy, rich, oil-cured black olives, extra-virgin olive oil, and lemon zest give these rustic cookies a fruity, olive taste. They make a delicious treat any time of day but have a short shelf-life of 1 or 2 days.

In a medium bowl, sift together flour, cornstarch, baking powder, and kosher salt. Whisk in cornmeal. Set aside.

In the large bowl of an electric mixer, with speed set to high, cream butter, sour cream, and olive oil for 1 to 2 minutes. Add sugar and egg. Beat 1 to 2 minutes, until smooth. Add lemon zest, and beat until combined.

Set mixer speed to low. Add flour mixture and mix until just combined.

Add olives; mix until combined. Place dough in covered bowl and chill for 1 hour, or overnight, until firm.

Preheat oven to 350 degrees. Line cookie sheets with parchment paper.

Using a small cookie scoop (#100), shape dough into 1-inch balls and drop onto prepared sheets, spacing them 2 inches apart. Using the bottom of a glass or back of a spoon, flatten the balls to $\frac{1}{3}$-inch thickness. Bake 12 to 14 minutes, until firm to the touch and bottoms are brown. Transfer cookies, still on parchment, to wire racks to cool completely.

Store in an airtight container, at room temperature, for up to 2 days.

INGREDIENTS

½ cup all-purpose flour
2 tbsp. cornstarch
⅛ tsp. baking powder
1/16 tsp. fine kosher salt
¼ cup finely ground cornmeal
2 tbsp. (¼ stick) unsalted butter, room temperature
2 tbsp. sour cream, room temperature
2 tsp. extra-virgin olive oil
2 tbsp. granulated sugar
1 large egg, room temperature
2 tsp. grated lemon zest, packed
¼ cup coarsely chopped, pitted, oil-cured black olives, rinsed lightly and patted dry

Baker's Note: Be careful not to overbake, as the olives may become bitter.

Savory Cheddar Cocktail Cookies
Makes 36 to 40 cookies

What better to munch on while watching the game than a savory cheddar cheese cookie? These cookies are delicious plain or "frosted" with one of the tangy, hot-pepper-jelly or bacon-cream-cheese toppings. They also make a great appetizer, served with your favorite beverage, or a wonderful accompaniment to soup or salad. I use fully cooked, packaged bacon, to minimize grease in my bacon toppings.

In a medium bowl, sift together flour and spices. Set aside.

In a food processor, combine cheddar cheese, parmesan cheese, and butter. Process until a creamy paste forms. Add egg yolk, and process until well blended. Add flour mixture, and pulse until soft dough forms. Refrigerate in a covered bowl for 1 to 2 hours, until firm.

Preheat oven to 350 degrees. Line cookie sheets with parchment paper.

Using a small cookie scoop (#100), shape dough into ¾-inch balls and drop onto prepared sheets, spacing them 1 inch apart. Using the bottom of a glass or back of a spoon, flatten the balls to ⅓-inch thickness. Bake 12 to 14 minutes, until golden brown. Cool on cookie sheets 2 minutes. Transfer cookies, still on parchment, to wire racks to cool completely.

Prepare toppings in 3 small separate bowls. Using a large spoon, mix ingredients for each topping until thoroughly combined. Refrigerate at least 30 minutes, for flavors to meld.

Prior to serving, return toppings to room temperature. Spread ½ tsp. on top of each cookie.

Store unfrosted cookies in an airtight container, at room temperature, for up to 5 days.

INGREDIENTS

1 cup all-purpose flour
¼ tsp. paprika
⅛ tsp. white pepper
⅛ tsp. cayenne pepper
1½ cups (about 6 oz.) shredded sharp cheddar cheese
½ cup (about 2 oz.) freshly grated parmesan cheese
8 tbsp. (1 stick) unsalted butter, room temperature
1 large egg yolk, room temperature

Hot-Pepper-Jelly Topping
½ cup cream cheese, room temperature
1½ tbsp. jalapeño hot-pepper jelly

Bacon-Horseradish Topping
½ cup cream cheese, room temperature
1 tbsp. sour cream, room temperature
2 tsp. prepared horseradish, room temperature
¼ cup fully cooked, finely chopped or crumbled bacon

Maple-Mustard-Bacon Topping
½ cup cream cheese, room temperature
1 tbsp. Dijon mustard
1 tbsp. maple syrup
¼ cup fully cooked, finely chopped or crumbled bacon

Baker's Note: Each topping recipe makes enough "frosting" for an entire cookie batch. Adjust amounts accordingly, if you plan to make more than 1 topping. Leftover toppings are great served on water crackers.

Green Peppercorn and Pink Sea Salt Wafers
Makes 24 to 30 cookies

Buttery Comte cheese, green peppercorns, and pink Himalayan sea salt create a complex flavor that makes these zesty cookies perfect for a before-dinner snack with a light, fruity wine. The peppery taste is mildly warm, not overbearing. If you like cheese straws, you will love these cookies.

In a medium bowl, sift together flour and salt. Whisk in peppercorns. Set aside.

In a food processor, pulse cheese and butter, until a creamy paste forms. Add flour mixture, and pulse until just combined. Mixture will be crumbly. Gather dough together, and place in a covered bowl. Chill overnight, for flavors to meld.

Preheat oven to 350 degrees. Line cookie sheets with parchment paper.

Using a small cookie scoop (#100), shape dough into ¾-inch balls and drop onto prepared sheets, spacing them 2 inches apart. Using the bottom of a glass or back of a spoon, flatten the balls to ¼-inch thickness. Sprinkle each cookie with a few grains of sea salt.

Bake 10 to 12 minutes, until edges are golden brown. Cool 2 minutes on cookie sheets. Transfer cookies, still on parchment, to wire racks to cool completely.

Store in an airtight container, at room temperature, for up to 5 days.

INGREDIENTS

¾ cup all-purpose flour

¼ tsp. fine pink Himalayan salt, plus extra for sprinkling

1½ tsp. crushed or ground green peppercorns

1 cup (about 3 oz.) grated Comte or aged Manchego cheese

6 tbsp. (¾ stick) unsalted butter, room temperature

Baker's Note: Substitute 1¼ tsp. peppercorn medley for green peppercorns, if desired.

Swiss Cheese and Mustard Puffs
Makes 30 to 36 cookies

These tangy, buttery, mustard-cheese biscuits make a great snack. With their light texture and delicious taste, it's easy to eat a handful. Try them with a crisp white wine or a cold beer.

In a medium bowl, sift together flour and salt. Set aside.

In a food processor, combine Swiss cheese and butter. Process until a creamy paste forms. Add mustards. Process until well blended.

Add flour. Pulse until just combined. Shape dough into a ¾-inch by 9-inch log. Wrap in plastic wrap or wax paper. Freeze for at least 2 hours, or overnight, until firm.

Preheat oven to 350 degrees. Line cookie sheets with parchment paper.

Cut log into ¼-inch-thick slices. Place slices 2 inches apart on prepared sheets. Bake 10 to 12 minutes, until edges are golden brown. Cool 2 minutes on cookie sheets. Transfer cookies, still on parchment, to wire racks to cool completely.

Store in an airtight container, at room temperature, for up to 5 days.

INGREDIENTS

½ cup all-purpose flour
¼ tsp. salt
1 cup (about 4 oz.) shredded Emmentaler Swiss cheese
4 tbsp. (½ stick) unsalted butter, room temperature
1 tbsp. Dijon mustard
½ tsp. dry mustard

Baker's Note: For a less mustardy cookie, reduce the mustards by half. For an extra kick, sift $\frac{1}{16}$ tsp. cayenne pepper into the flour mixture.

Tarragon-Lemon Cookies
Makes 30 to 36 cookies

Can cookies cleanse the palate? These can! Refreshingly light, these lemon and tarragon cookies are perfect anytime. These are my favorite herb cookies.

In a medium bowl, sift together flour and sea salt. Whisk in almond flour. Set aside.

In the large bowl of an electric mixer, with speed set to high, cream butter and sugar, about 2 minutes, until light and fluffy. Add olive oil, tarragon, lemon zest, and egg yolk. Beat about 2 minutes, until incorporated.

Reduce mixer speed to low. Add flour mixture. Mix until well combined and dough is smooth. Place in a covered bowl, and refrigerate 1 to 2 hours, or overnight, until firm.

Preheat oven to 350 degrees. Line cookie sheets with parchment paper.

Using a small cookie scoop (#100), shape dough into 1-inch balls and drop onto prepared sheets, spacing them 2 inches apart. Using the bottom of a glass or back of a spoon, flatten the balls to ⅓-inch thickness. Bake 12 to 14 minutes, until lightly browned. Cool on cookie sheets for 2 minutes. Transfer cookies, still on parchment, to wire racks to cool completely.

Store in an airtight container, at room temperature, for up to 3 days.

INGREDIENTS

¾ cup all-purpose flour
¼ tsp. fine sea salt
½ cup almond flour
4 tbsp. (½ stick) unsalted butter, room temperature
¼ cup granulated sugar
2 tbsp. extra-virgin olive oil
1 tbsp. finely chopped tarragon leaves
1 tsp. grated lemon zest, packed
1 large egg yolk, room temperature

Delicate but Feisty Sensations

Macarons and meringues are emerging as easy-to-make, delicious, gluten-free desserts, and elegant tuile and lace cookies are staging a comeback. This chapter presents some fanciful flavor combinations that transport these trendy, sophisticated cookies to a sassier, zestier place.

Lavender-Ginger Clouds
Makes 30 to 36 cookies, *gluten-free*

Culinary-grade lavender buds lend a subtle tangy, floral flavor and ginger gives a spicy kick to these unique meringues. You can find culinary-grade lavender in specialty herb or tea shops.

Preheat oven to 250 degrees. Line cookie sheets with parchment paper.

In the small bowl of a food processor, combine the sugars, lavender, and ginger. Pulse until lavender and ginger are finely ground.

In the small bowl of an electric mixer, with speed set to high, beat egg whites until foamy. Add salt and cream of tartar. Beat until soft peaks form. Add the lavender-sugar mixture, 1 tbsp. at a time, and beat until stiff peaks form. Set mixer speed to low, and mix in vanilla.

Drop or pipe double tsp. batter onto prepared cookie sheets, spacing 2 inches apart. Bake 30 to 35 minutes, until firm to the touch and tops are faintly cracked. Transfer cookies, still on parchment, to wire racks to cool completely.

Store in an airtight container, at room temperature, for up to 5 days.

INGREDIENTS

½ cup superfine sugar
¼ cup powdered sugar
1 tbsp. culinary-grade, dried lavender buds
2 tsp. finely chopped crystallized ginger
2 large egg whites, room temperature
⅛ tsp. salt
⅛ tsp. cream of tartar
¼ tsp. pure vanilla extract

Baker's Note: If making meringues on a humid day, add ¼ tsp. dried egg white with the salt and cream of tartar. The dried egg white will help the meringues hold their structure.

Green Tea Macarons with Almond Cream
Makes 30 to 40 unfilled cookies or 15 to 20 filled cookies, *gluten-free*

The herbal flavor of the powdered green tea mellows in the almond-sugar base and pairs nicely with the almond cream filling. If you prefer a tangy filling, try the white chocolate-crème fraiche ganache from the Chocolate Malt Sandwich Cookies recipe (see index). You can even serve the macarons without filling. Matcha is a powdered green tea that can be purchased at fine tea stores or online.

Preheat oven to 325 degrees. Line cookie sheets with parchment paper.

In a food processor, combine almond flour, powdered sugar, matcha, and salt. Pulse to make a fine powder. Set aside.

In the small bowl of an electric mixer, combine egg whites and cream of tartar. Set mixer speed to high, and beat until soft peaks form. Gradually add superfine sugar, and beat until stiff peaks form.

Turn off mixer. Using a rubber spatula, fold in almond mixture in 2 or 3 portions, folding after each portion but being careful not to deflate the batter. Mix until combined and no almond crumbs remain. Do not overmix, as this will cause cracking in the macarons.

Transfer batter to a pastry bag fitted with a ½-inch plain tip (#8) or a heavy-duty zip-sealed, plastic bag with a very small opening cut in 1 corner of the bag. Pipe 1-inch round cookies onto prepared cookie sheets, spacing them 2 inches apart. Lift each cookie sheet, and sharply rap down onto the countertop 3 or 4 times to flatten any peaks.

Bake 10 to 12 minutes, until firm to the touch and tops are shiny but not cracked. Cool completely on cookie sheets.

In the small bowl of an electric mixer, with speed set to low, beat almond paste. Add butter and sugar. Set speed to high. Beat until combined.

Add heavy cream and vanilla to the mixture. Beat until well combined. Chill filling in refrigerator for 10 minutes, until set.

On the flat side of a cookie, spread ½ tsp. filling. Place a second cookie, flat side down, on top of filling and gently press cookies together. Repeat with remaining cookies.

Refrigerate filled macarons in an airtight container for 12 hours before serving, so that the aroma of the filling infuses the cookies. Bring to room temperature before serving.

Store filled cookies in an airtight container, in the refrigerator, for up to 3 days.

INGREDIENTS

½ cup plus 2 tbsp. almond flour
⅓ cup plus 2 tbsp. powdered sugar
1½ tsp. matcha (green tea) powder
1/16 tsp. salt
2 large egg whites, room temperature
¼ tsp. cream of tartar
⅓ cup plus 2 tbsp. superfine sugar

Filling

¼ cup (about 2 oz.) almond paste
2 tbsp. (¼ stick) unsalted butter, room temperature
2 tbsp. superfine sugar
2 tbsp. heavy cream, room temperature
½ tsp. pure vanilla extract

Baker's Note: If you follow a gluten-free diet, check the label of the almond paste, as not all almond pastes are gluten free.

Saffron Pistachio Lace Cookies
Makes 72 to 80 cookies

You will be enchanted by these buttery wafer cookies, packed with pistachios and orange and infused with saffron. Their lacy texture is created by the sugar as it liquefies in baking. Saffron is an exotic spice harvested from crocus flowers. It is widely used in Spain, Italy, India, and the Middle East. For the best-quality saffron, choose threads that are dark red. Pair this cookie with mango ice cream or orange sorbet for an exotic dessert.

Melt butter over low heat. Remove from heat. Add saffron, and infuse for at least 5 minutes.

In a food processor, pulse pistachios and sugar until nuts are finely chopped but not ground. Set aside.

In a medium bowl, using a large spoon, stir together infused butter, pistachio-sugar mixture, almond extract, flour, orange zest, and orange juice. Cover bowl, and chill in refrigerator for 15 minutes.

Remove from refrigerator. Roll into two ½-inch by 9-inch logs (these cookies will spread a lot as they bake). Wrap logs in plastic wrap or wax paper, and freeze for at least 2 hours, or overnight, until firm.

Preheat oven to 325 degrees. Line cookie sheets with parchment paper.

Using a very sharp knife, slice 1 log into ¼-inch-thick slices. Place on prepared sheets 2 inches apart. Bake 8 to 10 minutes, watching carefully, until golden.

Immediately sprinkle each cookie with a few grains of sea salt, if desired. Transfer cookies, still on parchment, to wire racks to cool completely. Repeat with second log.

Store, layered between parchment or wax paper, in an airtight container, at room temperature, for up to 1 week.

INGREDIENTS

2½ tbsp. (⅓ stick) unsalted butter
⅛ tsp. crushed saffron threads (about .3 grams) (see Baker's Note)
¾ cup unsalted, shelled pistachios
½ cup granulated sugar
¼ tsp. pure almond extract
¼ cup all-purpose flour, sifted
2 tsp. grated orange zest, packed
2 tbsp. fresh orange juice
Fine sea salt for sprinkling (optional)

Baker's Note: Use a mortar and pestle to crush the saffron threads.

Raspberry-Lemon Meringues
Makes 30 to 36 cookies, *gluten-free*

These delicate-pink, flavor-packed meringues remind me of raspberry lemonade. I use Boyajian lemon oil and tart organic dried raspberries to give these cookies an extra punch (www.boyajianinc.com).

Preheat oven to 250 degrees. Line cookie sheets with parchment paper.

In the small bowl of a food processor, pulse raspberries until pulverized. Pass pulverized berries through a fine sieve to remove seeds. Discard seeds. Set aside.

In the small bowl of an electric mixer, with speed set to high, beat egg whites until foamy. Add salt and cream of tartar, and beat until soft peaks form. Add sugar, 1 tbsp. at a time, beating after each addition until stiff peaks form. Add lemon oil, and beat until thoroughly combined.

Turn off mixer. Sift dried berries over beaten egg whites. Using a rubber spatula, fold in berries, being careful not to deflate the batter.

Drop or pipe double tsp. batter onto prepared cookie sheets, spacing 2 inches apart. Bake 30 to 35 minutes. Transfer cookies, still on parchment, to wire racks to cool completely.

Store in an airtight container, at room temperature, for up to 3 days.

INGREDIENTS

⅓ cup freeze-dried raspberries
2 large egg whites, room temperature
⅛ tsp. salt
⅛ tsp. cream of tartar
½ cup plus 2 tbsp. superfine sugar
⅛ tsp. lemon oil (or substitute ¼ tsp. lemon extract plus ¼ tsp. grated lemon zest, packed)

Baker's Note: If you cannot find dried raspberries, substitute 2½ tbsp. red raspberry gelatin powder. Whisk gelatin with sugar before adding to egg-white mixture. Beat until gelatin is completely dissolved, 3 to 4 minutes. Meringues made with red raspberry gelatin will be bright pink.

Chocolate French Macarons with Red-Currant Buttercream
Makes 24 to 30 unfilled or 12 to 15 filled cookies, *gluten-free*

French macarons only recently arrived in U.S. bakeries, but they have been made for centuries in France. These light, chocolaty, gluten-free macarons are made with ground almonds, sugar, and egg whites and filled with a tangy red-currant buttercream. They are delicious eaten unfilled as well.

Preheat oven to 325 degrees. Line cookie sheets with parchment paper.

In a food processor, combine whole almonds, brown sugar, and ⅔ cup powdered sugar. Pulse until almonds are pulverized. Add remaining powdered sugar and cocoa. Pulse until well mixed. Set aside.

In the small bowl of an electric mixer, combine egg whites and cream of tartar. Set mixer speed to high, and beat until soft peaks form. Gradually add superfine sugar, and beat until stiff peaks form. Add vanilla, and mix until combined.

Turn off mixer. Using a rubber spatula, fold in almond mixture in 2 or 3 portions, folding after each portion but being careful not to deflate the batter. Mix until combined and no almond crumbs remain. Do not overmix, as this will cause cracking in the macarons.

Transfer batter to a pastry bag fitted with a ½-inch plain tip (#8) or a heavy-duty zip-sealed, plastic bag with a very small opening cut in 1 corner. Pipe 1-inch round cookies onto prepared cookie sheets, spacing them 2 inches apart. Lift each cookie sheet, and sharply rap down onto the countertop 3 or 4 times to flatten any peaks.

Bake 10 to 15 minutes, until firm to the touch and tops are shiny but not cracked. Cool completely on cookie sheets.

In the small bowl of an electric mixer, with speed set to high, beat egg and sugar, 2 to 3 minutes, until light and fluffy. Pour into a small saucepan, and add currant jelly. Heat over low flame, 2 to 3 minutes, stirring constantly until thick and creamy. Place in a small covered bowl, and cool in refrigerator for 10 minutes.

Clean blades and bowl. With speed set to medium, beat butter until fluffy. Add chilled mixture, and beat 1 to 2 minutes, until light and fluffy.

On the flat side of a cookie, spread ½ tsp. filling. Place a second cookie, flat side down, on top of filling and gently press cookies together. Repeat with remaining cookies.

Refrigerate filled macarons in an airtight container for 12 hours before serving, so that the aroma of the filling infuses the cookies. Bring to room temperature before serving.

Store filled cookies in an airtight container, in the refrigerator, for up to 3 days.

INGREDIENTS

½ cup whole blanched almonds
2 tbsp. packed light brown sugar
1 cup powdered sugar
3 tbsp. Dutch-process cocoa
2 large egg whites, room temperature
⅛ tsp. cream of tartar
2 tbsp. superfine sugar
1 tsp. pure vanilla extract

Filling
1 large egg, room temperature
⅓ cup superfine sugar
3 tbsp. red-currant jelly
8 tbsp. (1 stick) unsalted butter, room temperature

Grapefruit and Poppy-Seed Tuiles
Makes 60 to 72 cookies

These ruby-red grapefruit and poppy-seed cookies, with a texture reminiscent of fortune cookies, are a new take on traditional tuiles. You can leave the cookies flat or curve them. Bake them 1 sheet at a time, until you become efficient at shaping them as they come out of the oven.

In a medium bowl, combine sugar, egg whites, and salt. Using a wire whisk, beat until sugar is completely dissolved and egg white is foamy. Whisk in melted butter, until combined.

Whisk in flour, until combined. Add grapefruit zest and poppy seeds. Whisk until dispersed throughout the batter. Cover, and chill for at least 2 hours, to make the batter easier to manage.

Preheat oven to 350 degrees. Line cookie sheets with foil or a nonstick baking mat, such as Silpat. If using foil, smooth to remove any wrinkles, and lightly grease with extra melted butter.

Drop scant teaspoons of dough onto prepared cookie sheets, spacing 2 to 2½ inches apart. With a small angled spatula or the back of a spoon, spread batter evenly into ¹/₁₆-inch-thick, 1½- to 2-inch rounds or ovals. Bake 8 to 10 minutes, watching carefully, until golden brown around the edges but still pale in the centers.

For curved tuiles, cool 15 to 20 seconds on cookie sheet. Then, using an angled spatula, lift cookies 1 at a time, and drape over a rolling pin to curve. After 20 to 30 seconds, remove to wire rack to cool completely.

If cookies become too crisp to shape, return to oven for about 1 minute until pliable, and then shape. If you prefer the cookies flat, transfer cookies, still on foil or mat, to wire rack, and cool completely.

Store in an airtight container, at room temperature, for up to 2 days.

INGREDIENTS

⅓ cup plus 2 tbsp. granulated sugar
2 large egg whites, room temperature
¹/₁₆ tsp. salt
2 tbsp. (¼ stick) unsalted butter, melted and cooled slightly, plus extra for greasing foil
¼ cup plus 1 tbsp. all-purpose flour
1 tbsp. grated ruby-red grapefruit zest, packed
1½ tbsp. poppy seeds

Baker's Note: When using foil liners, try this curving shortcut recommended by award-winning cookbook author Alice Medrich. As soon as the cookies come out of the oven, carefully roll the foil liner into a bulky cylinder, with the cookies on the inside. After 2 or 3 minutes, carefully unroll it, and cool the cookies completely on the foil.

Chocolate-Orange Meringues
Makes 24 to 30 cookies, *gluten-free*

These double-chocolate meringue cookies are perfectly light and delicious, with a delightful hint of bitter orange. I love them served with chocolate ice cream.

Preheat oven to 275 degrees. Line cookie sheets with parchment paper.

In the small bowl of a food processor, combine cocoa and orange peel. Pulse until orange peel is finely ground and mixture resembles tiny cocoa nibs. Set aside.

In the small bowl of an electric mixer, with speed set to high, beat egg whites until foamy. Add cream of tartar and salt, and beat until soft peaks form. Add sugar, 1 tbsp. at a time, and beat until stiff peaks form. Add vanilla, and beat until combined. Turn off mixer. Using a rubber spatula, fold in cocoa mixture and chocolate in 2 portions, folding after each portion but being careful not to deflate the batter.

Drop or pipe double tsp. batter onto prepared sheets, spacing 2 inches apart. Bake 25 to 30 minutes, until tops are slightly brown and beginning to crack. Cool cookies completely on cookie sheets.

Store in an airtight container, at room temperature, for up to 5 days.

INGREDIENTS

1½ tbsp. Dutch-process cocoa
2 tbsp. finely chopped, candied orange peel
2 large egg whites, room temperature
1/16 tsp. cream of tartar
1/16 tsp. salt
⅔ cup superfine sugar
¼ tsp. pure vanilla extract
2 oz. finely chopped or grated semisweet or
  bittersweet chocolate

Index